HOW TO BE A SECONDARY SCHOOL SENCO

A Month by Month Guide

Gemma Corby

This book is dedicated to the memory of Antonia (Toni) Rodrigues.
Thank you for supporting me through my first SENCO role.

CONTENTS

ACRONYMS

SEND education has a ridiculous number of acronyms. I have attempted to list some of the more common ones below:

ADHD: Attention Deficit and Hyperactivity Disorder

ASC: Autistic Spectrum Condition (also known as ASD – Autistic Spectrum Disorder)

CAMHS – Child and Adolescent Mental Health Service

EHCP – Education and Healthcare Plan

EP – Educational Psychologist

HI – Hearing Impairment

IEP – Individual Education Plan

MLD – Moderate Learning Difficulty

MSI – Multi Sensory Impairment

OCD – Obsessive Compulsive Disorder

ODD – Oppositional Defiant Disorder

OT – Occupational Therapist/Therapy

PD – Physical Disability

PDA – Pathological Demand Avoidance

PT – Physiotherapist or Physiotherapy

PMLD – Profound and Multiple Learning Disabilities

SALT/SLT – Speech and Language Therapist/Therapy

SEMH – Social, Emotional and Mental Health

SLCN – Speech, Language and Communication Needs

SLD – Severe Learning Difficulty

SpLD – Specific Learning Difficulty (e.g. dyslexia)

TA – Teaching Assistant (sometimes LSA – Learning Support Assistant)

VI - Visual Impairment

INTRODUCTION

The role of SENCO is one of the most varied, rewarding and stimulating in a school. It is also incredibly demanding, and it can be isolating. If you are the SENCO in a conventional mainstream school, then you will most likely be the only one, with very few opportunities to meet and collaborate with other SENCOs. At times, it can feel like you are being pulled in all directions, the workload can feel overwhelming, with days where the pile of unfinished work is just so daunting you are not even sure where to begin. Since being appointed to my first SENCO role in 2015 I have quickly learnt how to prioritise, however it is not something that has necessarily come naturally to me. With this in mind I thought it would be useful to create a guide detailing the essential tasks that need to be completed each month. With a role as diverse and complex as SENCO it is not possible to include everything, after all one of the joys of the job is that no two days are the same - and good intentions can be quickly derailed by unexpected events that need to take priority. Yet, I felt it would still be helpful to know what the key tasks should be each month to ensure a productive and smooth academic year. This book is not an exhaustive list, but more of a guide to the most essential parts of the role of SENCO.

Structure of the Department

Before I go any further it is worth discussing the fundamentals behind a successful SEND department. I acknowledge that this will vary from setting to setting depending on a plethora of different factors: size of school, geographical location, demographics, but I think it's worth mentioning some essential points.

The SENCO's primary role should be being a SENCO. Not all schools recognise how complex the role is and think it can be tagged onto another role. In my experience, the least impactful SENCOs have been those who are too thinly spread. They may have a large teaching commitment or other responsibilities around the school. Ideally, the SENCO should be on the leadership team, or at very least have someone on the leadership team who is knowledgeable about supporting young people with additional needs and willing to act as an advocate for the SENCO at Senior Leadership Team meetings.

It is important that an adequate number of well-trained and capable teaching assistants (TAs) are on the SEND team. Ideally, each TA should have their own area of expertise. For example, you may have TAs with the following responsibilities: speech and language intervention, examination access arrangements, literacy intervention, numeracy intervention, communication and interaction skills intervention, mentoring etc. A well-trained, committed Lead TA (or Higher-Level TA) is a non-negotiable role, as they can act as a conduit between the TAs and the SENCO. As the SENCO role is very involved, it is not always possible for them to be available every moment of the day. The Lead TA can also have greater responsibilities, for example, acting as an assessor for examination access arrangements. This is an essential role, which is also complicated and time consuming. The Lead TA would have to undergo the necessary training to achieve Approved Practitioner Status (APS) and would need to be reliable and trustworthy.

Another vital member of any effective special needs team in a school is the SEND administrator. In my opinion, this is another non-negotiable role, as a SEND department would struggle to operate effectively without them. They are the person who is always there to answer phone calls from concerned parents. They are the person who is always there to offer a smile and friendly words of advice to anxious students. They are the person who supports the SENCO and the TAs, ensuring that everything flows efficiently and effectively. They are the thread that most often holds the whole SEND department together. As a SENCO you will need to learn to delegate work to the SEND administrator, otherwise you will run yourself ragged. Schools are generally drowning in paperwork, but the SEND department effectively faces a daily tsunami of bureaucracy. All SENCOs need someone organised, efficient and competent to support them and the department.

So, with the fundamentals in place, what does the SENCO role look like, month by month? It would be logical to start in September, seeing as that is the beginning of the academic year, however the key to a successful SEND department has to be preparation. With this is mind we will start in May.

MAY

T he second half of the summer term is the busiest in the SENCO's calendar. Yes, September is hectic, but if the groundwork is completed in the summer, then it becomes a lot more manageable.

Examinations

May is the start of the public examination season; therefore, the TA team will be busy supporting those with access arrangements. If this has been organised earlier in the year, then everything should run smoothly. As SENCO it is advisable to have a handle on how well things have gone, or have not gone, but really this is something that can be delegated to a trusted Lead TA, so the SENCO can get on with other important tasks.

Primary Preparation

This is key to a successful start in September. At this point in the year you should have a list of Year 6 students who will be imminently joining your school. Ask your admin support to contact each feeder school to request a list of all students with SEND and medical needs. Then, reach out to each school yourself, to arrange a visit. It is good practice to communicate with your fellow SENCOs, and it is a great opportunity to develop useful links. I aim to visit all of our feeder primary schools, who have children with additional needs, by mid-June. If there is a significant number of students with SEND joining the school, then it may not be possible for the SENCO to visit all the schools. If this is the case, send a trusted teaching assistant, possibly a Lead TA. You could do some visits together, so that they can observe how you would like the visits to run. It is advisable to take a form with you to complete, this will also act as a prompt to ensure all the essential information is collected. Additionally, create and take booklets outlining essential information about your school. These should include photographs of key members of staff and important rooms. A map and equipment list are also helpful, as is an exemplar timetable. This booklet can act as a helpful ice-breaker when meeting the young people for the first time. It is advisable to get the booklets made up and copied at the start of the month.

May is a good time of year for your admin support to send out letters to prospective parents detailing the key transition dates and any other information. You may wish to invite parents/carers to a coffee morning (see July), where they will have the opportunity to meet other parents/carers of young people with additional needs, both prospective and current. This is an excellent opportunity for parents/carers to ask questions in a relaxed and informal setting, as well as getting a parental perspective and hopefully making some links with others.

Policy Updates

Every year the SENCO has a statutory responsibility to review and update the SEND Information Report, which must be available on the school's website. The school's SEND Policy should be updated every three years (as long as the Information Report is updated annually), again this is a statutory requirement and needs to be available on the school's website. I find that May is a useful time to do this as I can link it into the budget plan for the year ahead, as I will know which services we will buying in from outside agencies, as well as our staffing structure.

JUNE

After each primary school visit it is advisable to convert your notes into a concise overview for teachers. Do this as soon as possible, whilst the information is fresh in your mind. It is also more manageable to write your notes up as you go along, to save on time. These notes will be essential reading for all teachers and TAs ahead of the new Year 6s coming to visit on their transition day (or week, as is the case in some schools). It is important to keep these notes as succinct as possible, as you don't want to overload your colleagues. Any emergency or medical information should be clearly highlighted (e.g. any severe allergies).

Additional Transition Day

Mid-June is the ideal time to hold an additional transition day for any Year 6s with special educational needs, or those whom their primary school feel would benefit from an extra day. I have received lots of positive feedback from running this additional day, as it helps to relieve some of the anxieties experienced by the young people, and their parents/carers. The day starts later than the usual school day, so that the Year 6s are not immediately overwhelmed by the frenetic atmosphere of a secondary school. Students, occasionally accompanied by their primary school TA, gather in the school canteen. This is a chance for them to meet each other, talk to the student leaders (usually Year 10s), sample some canteen food and meet with key members of staff. The day is run by the SENCO and the TA team, however other members of staff are encouraged to come and say hello. The Head of Year 7 and the Head Teacher should make a point of introducing themselves to the new cohort.

The day continues with a number of activities, including a fun exploration of the school with a TA and the student leaders. The Year 6s look for "clues" and complete the treasure hunt-style booklet they have been issued. They also have time to play some "getting-to-know-you" games, experience the lunchtime clubs that secondary school has to offer, including a games club (where the young people play traditional games, such as board games and card games) and Hideaway Club, specifically targeted at more vulnerable students. In the afternoon they complete a literacy task – which is made as fun as possible – and they play some numeracy games. Throughout the day we are able to informally assess their numeracy, literacy and social communication skills, which is really helpful when drawing up their Individual Education Plans (IEPs). The day draws to a close earlier than the usual school day, so that parents and carers can collect their young people, without the fear of there being large crowds. We emphasise to parents/carers that we are happy to arrange another visit to the school, if they think their child would benefit from this.

Outside Agencies

Once you have decided which outside agencies you will be working with for the forthcoming year, it is a good idea to plan ahead and secure dates in the diary, wherever appropriate. It may also be wise to meet to discuss the students you will want the professionals to work with, ahead of the mayhem of the new year. This is not always possible, depending on a number of factors - primarily the nature of the work to be carried out - but wherever you can, plan ahead (you should start to detect a theme here!). The time of the SENCO is precious, so preparation is essential.

Reading and Spelling Tests

June is a good time to conduct reading tests for all the Year 7s and Year 8s, as well as those Year 9s who received literacy intervention over the course of the academic year. This information will form the basis of future planning for intervention in the upcoming academic year, it will also highlight which interventions have/have not worked for individuals. It is important to have this information to hand, as it is imperative that you can justify the purpose of any intervention, after all, if it's not working, what's the point? However, in this era of austerity and constant belt-tightening, it seems more pertinent than ever before.

It is my belief that June is the ideal time to conduct these tests, as it is before the busyness and potential disruption experienced in July (school trips, sports day, transition week etc.), but it also means that the benefits of any intervention are fresh in the minds of the young people who participated, giving a more accurate reflection. Skills can easily become rusty over the course of the long summer holiday. This is true for any individual, adult or child; however, it can be even more pronounced in young people who experience difficulties with their memory.

Recruitment

It is not really possible to say when the perfect time is to consider recruiting teaching assistants to the SEND team, as it is a situation that could arise at any point in the year. However, more likely than not the summer term will be the time to recruit new members to your team. Make sure that the job description is clear – and that you highight which skills are essential, and which are desirable. I would personally prefer to recruit someone with good literacy and numeracy skills over lots of experience (if I had to choose – ideally, they would have experience too!). The application form and covering letter can give you some indication of a potential candidate's literacy skills, as well as their understanding of special educational needs.

Once you have selected a group of strong candidates, plan what you would like your interview process to look like. I would suggest: a tour of the school with reliable students; observing each of the candidates supporting in a lesson (perhaps just for 20 or 30 minutes of the lesson) - look to see how they relate to young people and how empathetic they are; an in-tray task (this is another good opportunity to assess their literacy skills, and understanding of the role) and finally a conventional interview with at least one other member of staff, being mindful to ensure that your interview panel includes someone who is safeguarding trained.

JULY

As the academic year draws to a close, it is an good time to contact the parents and carers of the new cohort of students with additional needs. If your school hosts any Year 6 transition events, it is vital that the SENCO attends and is clearly introduced. The SENCO needs to have a high profile, so that they can be easily sought out when necessary.

A coffee morning for parents and carers of new students, as well as the parents of current students has always proven to be a positive and productive way of developing supportive networks between the parents of children with additional needs. It also provides an opportunity for parents to ask a range of questions and get the perspective of both the school and other parents. Top tip: be mindful of any religious festivals, such as Ramadan, when parents and carers may be fasting.

When your school hosts its transition day/week, make sure that teachers and TAs have all the necessary SEND information for their new charges. Remember to carefully allocate TA support to the most vulnerable Year 6s. It is during this day/week that you could carry out the reading and spelling tests with the Year 6s, as this will provide you with time to mark them and plan intervention for the forthcoming year. There are two schools of thought on this, but I have found it useful to "hit the ground running", in terms of intervention in September. Stress to the students that this is information for the teachers; it is nothing they could have revised for and there is no need for them to be worried about it.

Administration

Not the most thrilling prospect, but it will pay dividends in the new academic year. Ensure that the Individual Education Plans (IEPs), or equivalent are written for the new Year 7s and that the rest of the IEPs are updated accordingly, alongside the SEND List (an overview of all the students in the school with additional needs). This is a really good opportunity to audit your SEND List and IEPs and ensure that everything is up to date and relevant. The updated IEPs and SEND List must be readily accessible to all teachers and teaching assistants, so they are able to plan for the year ahead. Archive any electronic copies of IEPs pertaining to students who have left the school, as you may be asked to send them onto their next education provider in September.

If you are fortunate to have a SEND administrator, sit down and work out the best days on which to hold the annual review meetings for the forthcoming year, so that a 'save the date' letter can be sent out well in advance. I will look at my new timetable and choose a day of the week where I have fewer (or ideally no) teaching commitments and will earmark two lessons for the reviews. Always block out two lessons, as some reviews can be quite involved, and you do not want to be rushing through such an important meeting. It is also useful to have some time following the meeting to write up any notes or action anything that needs actioning. This will also be a useful exercise for the SEND administrator, as they will be able to get on with organising the relevant paperwork and collecting staff comments in September.

Once the scores are in for the reading and spelling tests, it is possible to start planning intervention for next year. It may be the case that there are some students who have missed the tests and will need to be assessed in the new academic year, but you or your TA team can start penciling in interventions, and at least have a plan for the first cohort of students in September. Being organised in this way saves a lot of time and means that more students can receive the intervention they require.

Training

This is a good time of year to sit down with the member of staff in charge of whole school professional development to work out what SEND training needs to be delivered and on which dates this can potentially be achieved. It is wise to contact outside agencies at this point, should you wish them to provide some specialist training, so you can secure those in the calendar and plan what you specifically need them to deliver. Ideally, all whole school training days or sessions should include developing teachers' and TAs' knowledge of SEND. The SENCO should present during the first training day back following the summer holidays. This provides an opportunity for the school to set out its SEND vision, as well as addressing any practical concerns. For example, your school may have a new student starting with additional needs that are unfamiliar to most of the staff.

Access Arrangements

Throughout the month of July, Year 9 students who have received examination access arrangements should be formally assessed by the person in the school qualified to do so. This means that letters detailing any access arrangements can be sent home at the start of September and that the Form 8s can be completed and stored safely. Teachers and TAs can be made aware of who has access arrangements, so that students can start Year 10 with the correct provision in place. It is likely that throughout the course of the two GCSE years, other students requiring exam access arrangements will become apparant, which is why it is prudent to do as much as possible in advance.

Alternative End Of Term Arrangements

The end of the school year is usually a fun and exciting time, with the opportunity to do more off-timetable events, such as rewards trips or whole school fundraising events. However, some young people find the end of term very stressful. This is particularly true for those with a diagnosis of autism, but not exclusively so, as many others can find the change in routine and the frenetic feel to the end of term overwhelming. Some young people struggle with others wearing face paint, even if it is not a full-on transformation, this can prove to be an enormous distraction and can cause significant upset - particularly if the teachers join in! I am not about to propose that we ban this sort of frivolity, in some kind of Cromwellian move, but we do need to think how we can help our young people cope in these situations. It could be something as simple as encouraging the young person to use their time-out card and make use of a safe-space if they feel that their anxiety levels are increasing.

For some young people, just the thought of being in school when there is fancy-dress, or a special celebration in replacement of formal lessons, can cause such anxiety that their symptoms manifest themselves physiologically as well as emotionally. Some may suffer from an upset stomach or a nervous rash and may require medical support as well as emotional support. If you know that a student is particularly prone to an adverse reaction, it is prudent to plan for this and have alternative things for them to do away from the hubbub (for example, cooking, gardening or helping teachers and TAs with small jobs around the school).

If your school runs reward trips it is worth considering alternatives for students with additional needs, who may not cope with the proposed venue. Theme parks, whilst great fun for many students, can be the stuff of nightmares for others. Running alternative reward trips can be a solution, and they do not have to cost the Earth. For example, you could take a group of students for a walk around the local area, stopping off at various points of interest.

SEPTEMBER

To save myself from sleepless nights, I tend to come into school for a few days at the end of August. This allows me to get ahead of myself, as well as acting as a reminder of what I do for a living (and recalling simple things such as passwords!). I am not suggesting that this is for everybody, as we are all entitled to our holiday, but I have found it to be a good investment of time and it has meant I can leave on time for the first couple of weeks in September. My priority during this time is to email out the most up to date version of the SEND List (stressing that it is highly confidential – and should not be printed out and left where prying eyes may find it). I also ensure that teachers are reminded where the IEPs are, to help inform their planning.

Once September is here and our SEND administrator has returned, we will ensure that formal annual review letters are sent out, detailing the date, time and location of the meeting. It is also useful to set calendar reminders for when feedback is required from teachers and TAs. As everyone is very busy, it is essential that you support your colleagues by giving them plenty of notice. Other professionals will need to be invited to the annual review meeting as necessary. I find it useful to liaise with our careers advisor during this time too, so they know which Year 11 SEND students are a priority in the autumn term, as well as the Year 9s and Year 10s who will need advice on GCSE options and work experience, respectively.

Training

Hopefully, back in July you would have secured your slot for the initial training day following the summer holidays. This is a good opportunity to refresh your colleagues on the basics of SEND provision i.e. where to locate the IEPs, what their statutory duties are, what training will be on offer throughout the year, which outside agencies the school will be working with, what the plethora of acronyms actually mean etc. This can be a particularly useful exercise for new members of staff and NQTs, however everyone can benefit from a refresher. This will also be the ideal opportunity to provide training on any new students with unfamiliar and/or complex additional needs.

During your first meeting with the SEND team, it may be worth carrying out a training audit amongst the teaching assistants. Find out in which areas they feel confident in and where they could do with greater, more specific training. Ensure that this is organised throughout the course of the year and that the TAs are given the dates for any after school training by the end of September.

Intervention

Based on the reading and spelling data acquired in the summer term, start any intervention sessions as soon as possible. Ensure that any students who missed the assessments in the summer term are tested and that intervention for the whole of the forthcoming academic years is pencilled in.

Data

This is a good time of year to take stock of what the SEND profile of your school looks like. You may wish to use the four categories as stated in the SEND Code of Practice: Communication and Interaction; Cognition and Learning; Sensory and/or Physical and Social, Emotional and Mental Health Needs (focus on the primary need – as some young people will have multiple needs). You may also want to go into more specific detail – e.g. how many students have a diagnosis of dyslexia or ADHD? The first inset day after the summer holiday is a great opportunity to share this information with colleagues.

You should also have all of your reading and spelling data by the end of September and it is definitely a good idea to share this with teachers and TAs. Study this data closely to see if there are any significant improvements for individuals and consider if the literacy intervention that is in place for them is working. Do the same for all students receiving numeracy intervention.

OCTOBER

An important date in the calendar of all secondary schools is the annual open evening for prospective students and their parents/carers. It is an excellent opportunity for young people with additional needs to visit a range of secondary schools. For those students with an Education and Healthcare Plan (EHCP), the search may begin in Year 5, as the new school will need to be included on the amended plan.

It is imperative that the SEND department has an appropriate and easily accessible room on open evening. It should be welcoming and have adequate space, should sensitive or private conversations need to take place. Print out information gathering forms, so that you can record any conversations which you may benefit from referring to in the future, and store these safely. Make sure that all the different interventions carried out by the SEND department are represented, so that parents and carers are aware of what you have to offer in terms of support. Have tangible examples of what these interventions are – for example make any literacy programme resources available for parents/carers to explore (e.g. Sound Discovery, Catch Up Literacy and Lexia), alongside other interventions such as numeracy (e.g. Catch Up Numeracy programme, supported with Numicon resources), communication and interaction skills, mentoring, speech and language therapy, amongst others. The SENCO should of course be available, as should any lead teaching assistants.

Annual Reviews

The annual reviews should ideally start in October, as this gives students (and staff!) a couple of weeks to settle back in. Starting with Year 11 is advisable, as their teachers will already have a good idea of how they are coping with the demands of the course from their performance in Year 10. Also, Year 11 should be a priority as their EHCP will need to be amended regarding their post-16 provider. It is an opportunity to have important discussions regarding next steps and planning for the future. If your school has a sixth form, you may wish to start with Year 13. Each school has a different way of scheduling their annual reviews, but having trialled different methods, I found this to be the most effective:

October - November	Year 11 and Year 13	November - December	Year 7 and Year 9
January	Year 9 and Year 8	February	Year 8 and Year 12
March	Year 12 and Year 10	April	Year 10

Ensure that you give yourself or the SEND administrator adequate time to gather everyone's views prior to the review meeting. Leave a bit of wiggle room at the start and end of each new term, should anyone need to re-arrange the date of their young person's review. This will hopefully prevent you from having multiple reviews in one week and will give you some breathing space in terms of writing up the final review to send off to the local authority. Aim to have all the annual reviews completed by the end of the Spring Term, so that the Summer Term can be dedicated to the transition of students to Year 7 and from Year 11 (and Year 13). With this in mind, it is worth contacting primary schools in October to see if they would like the secondary school SENCO to attend any Year 5 or 6 annual review meetings.

NOVEMBER

The start of November is a good time to find out how the Year 7s have settled in following their first half term at secondary school. If your school has a parents' evening or equivalent, then this is the perfect opportunity. It is reassuring for the parents of young people with additional needs to touch base, even if there isn't anything in particular that they wish to discuss. It is also a chance for parents/carers with any concerns about their child's progress to meet with the SENCO. I have often found it to be a revealing and useful exercise. November is also a good time for the Year 7 annual reviews to take place, as well as the Year 9 reviews. At this stage in the academic year, the Year 9s will be considering their GCSE options, and what they want to do in Key Stage Four and possibly beyond. It is therefore important to include a transition plan (from Key Stage Three to Key Stage Four) within the Year 9 annual review meetings. This will form part of the statutory paperwork as well.

Updates

By this point in the autumn term, you should have an idea of who will be doing what intervention, at least for the bulk of the year ahead, if not the entire year (you may wish to leave some room for manoeuvre, as you never know who might require additional support at a later part of the year). Once you have all of this information, update your provision map/intervention schedule. Not only is this useful in terms of forward planning, it is also helpful to know what provision students have had retrospectively. For example, when applying for EHCP assessments for individuals, I will always refer to the provision maps from previous years to inform me. I have found this invaluable, as it is impossible to re-member all the intervention each and every student has had.

This may also be a good time of year to make contact with your school's SEND governor. This person can be a useful ally, so it is prudent to stay in regular contact. Also, the SENCO will need to report back to the governors, so the more you are in contact with your school's SEND governor, the less pressure there will be when you have to provide your feedback, as they will already be in the loop and have an understanding of how the department is operating.

DECEMBER

Just like the end of the summer term, the final days of the autumn term can be overwhelming and confusing for some students. For most people in the school, Christmas is an exciting time of year, but for some individuals it can cause a significant amount of stress; particularly for those with autism and/or sensory issues. It is essential to talk through any potential changes, such as non-uniform day, concerts, special performances etc. with any young person likely to be affected by disruption to the norm. Some students find Christmas jumper day challenging because it is a change and does not follow the school rules. Social Stories™ can be used to help break down some of these potential fears.

Not all staff will be aware of the negative impact that the festivities of Christmas can have on some students. Ensure that they know that sensory overload can cause stress, impacting individuals' levels of resilience and therefore their behaviour. Whilst it is essential that young people are encouraged to be flexible in their thinking and to be open-minded to changes, it is always useful to have a contingency plan for those who are not quite ready to do this. Rather than leaving them to feel excluded by sitting out, provide alternative treats, for example some of our students like to play card and board games, others enjoy watching films or doing mindful colouring-in.

College/University Applications

This is a sensible time to check how Year 11 and Year 13 students are progressing with their college and university applications. It may be useful to arrange a session with them (either with yourself, the careers advisor, or a teaching assistant) to go through any application forms and answer any questions they may have. It is also important to liaise with parents/carers during this time. Encourage the young people to visit as many education providers as possible and to always have a contingency plan, should they not get the grades they require.

JANUARY

The start of the new year is a natural time to review what has been put in place. Check that interventions are getting the desired results, and that the dates and times scheduled for any outside agencies are appropriate. Liaise with outside agencies to ensure that they are satisfied with the arrangements in place.

Observations

Throughout the Spring Term I aim to observe all of our TAs, in a lesson of their choice. We then meet the next day and go through what was effective and any areas for development (plus any training requirements, that may have been missed during the skills audit in September). It is also an opportunity to catch up with each and every TA on a one to one basis, without the constraints of a performance management meeting. In my experience, rather than the TAs being nervous or resistant to me observing them, they have embraced it and have been keen to show what they do. The feedback I received was that they felt more valued as a result. It is also incredibly helpful for me to see where the strengths of our department lie and where the areas for development are. Ideally, TA observations will take place annually.

FEBRUARY

I t is around this time of year that most Year 9 students will be considering their GCSE options. This is a potentially stressful time for many students, however for those with additional needs it can be even more so. Ensure that any young person with an EHCP has access to the careers advisor around this time and be prepared to liaise more regularly with anxious parents and carers. It may be worth offering young people with additional needs the option of doing one fewer GCSE, so they can have the time to focus on their other subjects. The groups should be small (no more than eight) and students should have access to computers; they can be run by Lead TAs, with the support of the SENCO where required. Usually, students have five periods over a fortnight to complete homework tasks, revise what they have learnt in lessons and prepare for assessments – as well as having time to focus on work experience and college applications when relevant. I have found these sessions to be invaluable in relieving the pressure of doing a full quota of GCSEs. Not all parents/carers are aware of what these sessions are about, so it is essential that the SENCO is available at the Year 9 Options Evening to promote and discuss this possibility – although it should be made clear that this subject is by invitation only - as to target the neediest students.

Important Dates

February is the final deadline to process applications for examination access arrangements using Access Arrangements Online (AAO). Check that everything is in place and that all the paperwork is complete, and that parents/carers have been formally informed in writing. The paperwork should be kept in a secure but accessible location, should it be required by the examination inspector.

This is also a good time to start thinking ahead in terms of the imminent transition of Year 6 students to secondary school. Send out a "dates for the diary" notification to all primary schools – so they can share it with any parents or carers who may find it useful. This could include:

Event	Date
Additional Transition Day	Mid-June
Year 6 Evening	Early July
Coffee Morning for Parents/ Carers	Mid-July
Year 6 Transition Day/Week	End of July
Open Evening (for Year 5 parents/ carers)	Early October

MARCH

With the public examinations just around the corner, it is worth brushing up on the rules and regulations for supporting students during their exams (i.e. by acting as a scribe, reader, practical assistant etc), as well as organising invigilator training. The SEND department, examinations officer and invigilation team can join forces to undertake training together. This can be done online, using video tutorials. It is not usually the most inspiring training, but it is practical and necessary, and means that everyone feels confident in their role.

Primary Focus

Continue to reach out to primary school colleagues. This is a busy time of year for them as the SATs approach, so it may not always be easy to get a quick response. By starting early with gentle reminders, you are more likely to have the information you require by May, assisting you in your transition planning. Ask your SEND administrator to send out the paperwork you require your primary counterpart to complete and make sure that you give a reasonable deadline for its return. You could also ask if you should be meeting with any outside agencies regarding Year 6 students; for example, if you have a young person with a hearing impairment joining your school, it would be advisable to meet with their specialist teacher (alongside their family) as soon as possible.

APRIL

Double check that all students are aware of their examination access arrangements, and that they continue to reflect their "usual way of working" (this phrase is key according to JCQ (Joint Council for Qualifications) guidelines). For example, some students may have stopped using a computer as their normal way of working, preferring to write by hand – or visa versa.

Ensure that all TAs are familiar with the access arrangements (teachers should be updated regularly throughout the course of the year), so they know how to support students correctly. Small cards detailing an individual's access arrangements can be created, for students to place on their desk during the examinations. These cards are helpful as they outline which access arrangements are in place at a glance.

Primary School Reminders

There is the risk that your primary school colleagues will be sick of the sight of your school's name appearing in their email inbox by the time you get to the summer term, but it is vital that you maintain contact with them. It really is a busy and stressful time for most primary schools, so it is easy to let things slide, even with the best intentions.

FINAL NOTE

As I mentioned in the introduction, this book is not intended to be an exhaustive list of everything a SENCO is required to do over the course of the year, but it does cover the essentials. If you follow this guide, your school will be compliant with the relevant legislation and taking the right steps to protect and support some of the most vulnerable young people. However, as anyone who has worked in a SEND department will testify, there is so much more to the role of SENCO and there will be plenty of curve balls with the potential to throw you off course. Being organised and collaborating with colleagues and parents/carers, as well as the young people themselves, are essential to running a successful SEND department. It can be hard work, but it is always rewarding.

ABOUT THE AUTHOR

Gemma Corby

 Gemma is a qualified teacher and special educational needs coordinator, based in Liverpool. She has taught in schools in Cambridgeshire, Aberdeen, London and Norfolk, and has been a regular contributor to the TES (Times Educational Supplement) since 2017. Gemma has several years experience as a SENCO, and is currently head of a SEND department in a Merseyside secondary school.

HOW TO BE A SECONDARY SCHOOL SENCO

Printed in Great Britain
by Amazon

82890773R00031